GW00499969

NFT

A Complete Guide to NFT for Beginners.

Sam Nakamoto

© Copyright 2020 - All rights reserved.

The content contained within this book may not be reproduced, duplicated or transmitted without direct written permission from the author or the publisher.

Under no circumstances will any blame or legal responsibility be held against the publisher, or author, for any damages, reparation, or monetary loss due to the information contained within this book. Either directly or indirectly.

Legal Notice:

This book is copyright protected. This book is only for personal use. You cannot amend, distribute, sell, use, quote or paraphrase any part, or the content within this book, without the consent of the author or publisher.

Disclaimer Notice:

Please note the information contained within this document is for educational and entertainment purposes only. All effort has been executed to present accurate, up to date, and reliable, complete information. No warranties of any kind are declared or implied. Readers acknowledge that the author is not engaging in the rendering of legal, financial, medical or professional advice. The content within this book has been derived from various sources. Please consult a licensed professional before attempting any techniques outlined in this book.

By reading this document, the reader agrees that under no circumstances is the author responsible for any losses, direct or indirect, which are incurred as a result of the use of information contained within this document, including, but not limited to, — errors, omissions, or inaccuracies.

TABLE OF CONTENT

INTRODUCTION

There's nothing like an explosion of blockchain news to leave you thinking, "Um… what's going on here?" That's the feeling I've experienced while reading about Grimes getting millions of dollars for NFTs or about Nyan Cat being sold as one. And by the time we all thought we sort of knew what the deal was, the founder of Twitter put an autographed tweetup for sale as an NFT.

You might be wondering: what is an NFT, anyhow?

After literal hours of reading, I think I know. I also think I'm going to cry.

Okay, let's start with the basics.

What is Blockchain?

Blockchain seems complicated, and it definitely can be, but its core concept is really quite simple. A blockchain is a type of database. To be able to understand blockchain, it helps to first understand what a database actually is.

A database is a collection of information that is stored electronically on a computer system. Information, or data, in databases is typically structured in table format to allow for easier searching and filtering for specific information. What is the difference between someone using a spreadsheet to store information rather than a database?

Spreadsheets are designed for one person, or a small group of people, to store and access limited amounts of information. In contrast, a database is designed to house significantly larger amounts of information that can be accessed, filtered, and manipulated quickly and easily by any number of users at once.

Large databases achieve this by housing data on servers that are made of powerful computers. These servers can sometimes be built using hundreds or thousands of computers in order to have the computational power and storage capacity necessary for many users to access the database simultaneously. While a spreadsheet or database may be accessible to any number of people, it is often owned by a business and managed by an appointed individual that has complete control over how it works and the data within it.

So how does a blockchain differ from a database?

Storage Structure

One key difference between a typical database and a blockchain is the way the data is structured. A blockchain collects information together in groups, also known as blocks, that hold sets of information. Blocks have certain storage capacities and, when filled, are chained onto the previously filled block, forming a chain of data known as the "blockchain." All new information that follows that freshly added block is compiled into a newly formed block that will then also be added to the chain once filled.

A database structures its data into tables whereas a blockchain, like its name implies, structures its data into chunks (blocks) that are chained together. This makes it so that all blockchains are databases but not all databases are blockchains. This system also inherently makes an irreversible timeline of data when implemented in a decentralized nature. When a block is filled it is set in stone and becomes a part of this timeline. Each block in the chain is given an exact timestamp when it is added to the chain.

Transaction Process

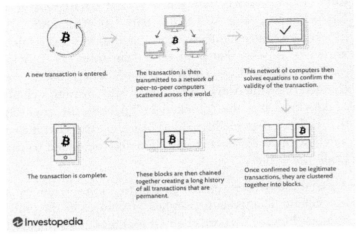

A new transaction is entered.

The transaction is then transmitted to a network of peer-to-peer computers scattered across the world.

This network of computers then solves equations to confirm the validity of the transaction.

The transaction is complete.

These blocks are then chained together creating a long history of all transactions that are permanent.

Once confirmed to be legitimate transactions, they are clustered together into blocks.

Investopedia

Attributes of Cryptocurrency

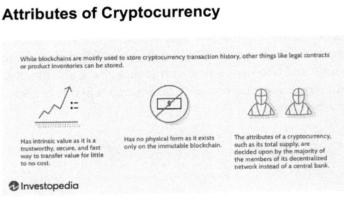

While blockchains are mostly used to store cryptocurrency transaction history, other things like legal contracts or product inventories can be stored.

Has intrinsic value as it is a trustworthy, secure, and fast way to transfer value for little to no cost.

Has no physical form as it exists only on the immutable blockchain.

The attributes of a cryptocurrency, such as its total supply, are decided upon by the majority of the members of its decentralized network instead of a central bank.

Investopedia

Decentralization

For the purpose of understanding blockchain, it is instructive to view it in the context of how it has been implemented by Bitcoin. Like a database, Bitcoin needs a collection of computers to store its blockchain. For Bitcoin, this blockchain is just a specific type of database that stores every Bitcoin transaction ever made. In Bitcoin's case, and unlike most databases, these computers are not all under one roof, and each computer or group of computers is operated by a unique individual or group of individuals.

Imagine that a company owns a server comprised of 10,000 computers with a database holding all of its client's account information. This company has a warehouse containing all of these computers under one roof and has full control of each of these computers and all the information contained within them. Similarly, Bitcoin consists of thousands of computers, but each computer or group of computers that hold its blockchain is in a different geographic location and they are all operated by separate individuals or groups of people. These computers that makeup Bitcoin's network are called nodes.

In this model, Bitcoin's blockchain is used in a decentralized way. However, private, centralized blockchains, where the computers that make up its network are owned and operated by a single entity, do exist.

In a blockchain, each node has a full record of the data that has been stored on the blockchain since its inception. For Bitcoin, the data is the entire history of all Bitcoin transactions. If one node has an error in its data it can use the thousands of other nodes as a reference point to correct itself. This way, no one node within the network can alter information held within it. Because of this, the history of transactions in each block that make up Bitcoin's blockchain is irreversible.

If one user tampers with Bitcoin's record of transactions, all other nodes would cross-reference each other and easily pinpoint the node with the incorrect information. This system helps to establish an exact and transparent order of events. For Bitcoin, this information is a list of transactions, but it also is possible for a blockchain to hold a variety of information like legal contracts, state identifications, or a company's product inventory.

In order to change how that system works, or the information stored within it, a majority of the decentralized network's computing power would need to agree on said changes. This ensures that whatever changes do occur are in the best interests of the majority.

Transparency

Because of the decentralized nature of Bitcoin's blockchain, all transactions can be transparently viewed by either having a personal node or by using blockchain explorers that allow anyone to see transactions occurring live. Each node has its own copy of the chain that gets updated as fresh blocks are confirmed and added. This means that if you wanted to, you could track Bitcoin wherever it goes.

For example, exchanges have been hacked in the past where those who held Bitcoin on the exchange lost everything. While the hacker may be entirely anonymous, the Bitcoins that they extracted are easily traceable. If the Bitcoins that were stolen in some of these hacks were to be moved or spent somewhere, it would be known.

Is Blockchain Secure?

Blockchain technology accounts for the issues of security and trust in several ways. First, new blocks are always stored linearly and chronologically. That is, they are always added to the "end" of the blockchain. If you take a look at Bitcoin's blockchain, you'll see that each block has a position on the chain, called a "height." As of November 2020, the block's height had reached 656,197 blocks so far.

After a block has been added to the end of the blockchain, it is very difficult to go back and alter the contents of the block unless the majority reached a consensus to do so. That's because each block contains its own hash, along with the hash of the block before it, as well as the previously mentioned time stamp. Hash codes are created by a math function that turns digital information into a string of numbers and letters. If that information is edited in any way, the hash code changes as well.

Here's why that's important to security. Let's say a hacker wants to alter the blockchain and steal Bitcoin from everyone else. If they were to alter their own single copy, it would no longer align with everyone else's copy. When everyone else cross-references their copies against each other, they would see this one copy stand out and that hacker's version of the chain would be cast away as illegitimate.

Succeeding with such a hack would require that the hacker simultaneously control and alter 51% of the copies of the blockchain so that their new copy becomes the majority copy and thus, the agreed-upon chain. Such an attack would also require an immense amount of money and resources as they would need to redo all of the blocks because they would now have different timestamps and hash codes.

Due to the size of Bitcoin's network and how fast it is growing, the cost to pull off such a feat would probably be insurmountable. Not only would this be extremely expensive, but it would also likely be fruitless. Doing such a thing would not go unnoticed, as network members would see such drastic alterations to the blockchain. The network members would then fork off to a new version of the chain that has not been affected.

This would cause the attacked version of Bitcoin to plummet in value, making the attack ultimately pointless as the bad actor has control of a worthless asset. The same would occur if the bad actor were to attack the new fork of Bitcoin. It is built this way so that taking part in the network is far more economically incentivized than attacking it.

What Is A Nft? What Does Nft Stand For?

Non-fungible token.

That doesn't make it any clearer.

Right, sorry. "Non-fungible" more or less means that it's unique and can't be replaced with something else. For example, a bitcoin is fungible — trade one for another bitcoin, and you'll have exactly the same thing. A one-of-a-kind trading card, however, is non-fungible. If you traded it for a different card, you'd have something completely different. You gave up a Squirtle, and got a 1909 T206 Honus Wagner, which *StadiumTalk* calls "the Mona Lisa of baseball cards." (I'll take their word for it.)

How do NFTs work?

At a very high level, most NFTs are part of the Ethereum blockchain. Ethereum is a cryptocurrency, like bitcoin or dogecoin, but its blockchain also supports these NFTs, which store extra information that makes them work differently from, say, an ETH coin. It is worth noting that other blockchains can implement their own versions of NFTs. (Some already have.)

What's worth picking up at the NFT supermarket?

NFTs can really be anything digital (such as drawings, music, your brain downloaded and turned into an AI), but a lot of the current excitement is around using the tech to sell digital art.

You mean, like, people buying my good tweets?

I don't think anyone can stop you, but that's not really what I meant. A lot of the conversation is about NFTs as an evolution of fine art collecting, only with digital art.

(Side note, when coming up with the line "buying my good tweets," we were trying to think of something so silly that it wouldn't be a real thing. So *of course* the founder of Twitter would take a shot at it just days after we posted the article.)

Do people really think this will become like art collecting?

I'm sure some people really hope so — like whoever paid almost $390,000 for a 50-second video by Grimes or the person who paid $6.6 million for a video by Beeple.

Wow, rude. But yeah, that's where it gets a bit awkward. You can copy a digital file as many times as you want, including the art that's included with an NFT.

But NFTs are designed to give you something that can't be copied: ownership of the work (though the artist can still retain the copyright and reproduction rights, just like with physical artwork). To put it in terms of physical art collecting: anyone can buy a Monet print. But only one person can own the original.

No shade to Beeple, but the video isn't really a Monet.

What do you think of the $3,600 Gucci Ghost? Also, you didn't let me finish earlier. That image that Beeple was auctioning off at Christie's ended up selling for $69 million, which, by the way, is $15 million more than Monet's painting Nymphéas sold for in 2014.

Whoever got that Monet can actually appreciate it as a physical object. With digital art, a copy is literally as good as the original.

But the *flex* of owning an original Beeple...

What's the point?

That really depends on whether you're an artist or a buyer.

I'm an artist.

First off: I'm proud of you. Way to go. You might be interested in NFTs because it gives you a way to sell work that there otherwise might not be much of a market for. If you come up with a really cool digital sticker idea, what are you going to do? Sell it on the iMessage App Store? No way.

Also, NFTs have a feature that you can enable that will pay you a percentage every time the NFT is sold or changes hands, making sure that if your work gets super popular and balloons in value, you'll see some of that benefit.

I'm a buyer.

One of the obvious benefits of buying art is it lets you financially support artists you like, and that's true with NFTs (which are way trendier than, like, Telegram stickers). Buying an NFT also usually gets you some basic usage rights, like being able to post the image online or set it as your profile picture. Plus, of course, there are bragging rights that you own the art, with a blockchain entry to back it up.

No, I meant I'm a *collector*.

Ah, okay, yes. NFTs can work like any other speculative asset, where you buy it and hope that the value of it goes up one day, so you can sell it for a profit. I feel kind of dirty for talking about that, though.

So every NFT is unique?

In the boring, technical sense that every NFT is a unique token on the blockchain. But while it could be like a van Gogh, where there's only one definitive actual version, it could also be like a trading card, where there's 50 or hundreds of numbered copies of the same artwork.

Who would pay hundreds of thousands of dollars for what basically amounts to a trading card?

Well, that's part of what makes NFTs so messy. Some people treat them like they're the future of fine art collecting (read: as a playground for the mega-rich), and some people treat them like Pokémon cards (where they're accessible to normal people but also a playground for the mega-rich). Speaking of Pokémon cards, Logan Paul just sold some NFTs relating to a million-dollar box of the—

Please stop. I hate where this is going.

Yeah, he sold NFT video clips, which are just clips from a video you can watch on YouTube anytime you want, for up to $20,000. He also sold NFTs of a Logan Paul Pokémon card.

Who paid $20,000 for a video clip of Logan Paul?!

A fool and their money are soon parted, I guess?

It would be hilarious if Logan Paul decided to sell 50 more NFTs of the exact same video.

Linkin Park's Mike Shinoda (who also sold some NFTs that included a song) actually talked about that. It's totally a thing someone could do if they were, in his words, "an opportunist crooked jerk." I'm not saying that Logan Paul is that, just that you should be careful who you buy from.

Can I buy this article as an NFT?

No, but technically anything digital could be sold as an NFT. deadmau5 has sold digital animated stickers. William Shatner has sold Shatner-themed trading cards (one of which was apparently an X-ray of his teeth).

Gross. Actually, could I buy someone's teeth as an NFT?

There have been some attempts at connecting NFTs to real-world objects, often as a sort of verification method. Nike has patented a method to verify sneakers' authenticity using an NFT system, which it calls CryptoKicks. But so far, I haven't found any teeth, no. I'm scared to look.

Look? Where?

There are several marketplaces that have popped up around NFTs, which allow people to buy and sell. These include OpenSea, Rarible, and Grimes' choice, Nifty Gateway, but there are plenty of others.

I've heard there were kittens involved. Tell me about the kittens.

NFTs really became technically possible when the Ethereum blockchain added support for them as part of a new standard. Of course, one of the first uses was a game called CryptoKitties that allowed users to trade and sell virtual kittens. Thank you, internet.

I love kittens.

Not as much as the person who paid over $170,000 for one.

My face when I'm worth $170K. Image: Cryptokitties.co

Arrrrrggggg!

Same. But in my opinion, the kittens show that one of the most interesting aspects of NFTs (for those of us not looking to create a digital dragon's lair of art) is how they can be used in games. There are already games that let you have NFTs as items. One even sells virtual plots of land as NFTs. There could be opportunities for players to buy a unique in-game gun or helmet or whatever as an NFT, which would be a flex that most people could actually appreciate.

Could I pull off a museum heist to steal NFTs?

That depends. Part of the allure of blockchain is that it stores a record of each time a transaction takes place, making it harder to steal and flip than, say, a painting hanging in a museum. That said, cryptocurrencies have been stolen before, so it really would depend on how the NFT is being stored and how much work a potential victim would be willing to put in to get their stuff back.

Note: Please don't steal.

Should I be worried about digital art being around in 500 years?

Probably. Bit rot is a real thing: image quality deteriorates, file formats can't be opened anymore, websites go down, people forget the password to their wallets. But physical art in museums is also shockingly fragile.

I want to maximize my blockchain use. Can I buy NFTs with cryptocurrencies?

Yes. Probably. A lot of the marketplaces accept Ethereum. But technically, anyone can sell an NFT, and they could ask for whatever currency they want.

Will trading my Logan Paul NFTs contribute to global warming and melt Greenland?

It's definitely something to look out for. Since NFTs use the same blockchain technology as some energy-hungry cryptocurrencies, they also end up using a lot of electricity. There are people working on mitigating this issue, but so far, most NFTs are still tied to cryptocurrencies that generate a lot of greenhouse gas emissions. There have been a few cases where artists have decided to not sell NFTs or to cancel future drops after hearing about the effects they could have on climate change. Thankfully, one of my colleagues has really dug into it, so you can read this piece to get a fuller picture.

Can I build an underground art cave / bunker to store my NFTs?

Well, like cryptocurrencies, NFTs are stored in digital wallets (though it is worth noting that the wallet does specifically have to be NFT-compatible). You could always put the wallet on a computer in an underground bunker, though.

Are you tired of typing "NFT"?

Yes.

Update March 5th, 8:07PM ET: Added the news that Jack Dorsey was selling one of his tweets as an NFT because I originally made a joke and cannot believe it actually happened.

Update March 11th, 1:42PM ET: Added the news that Beeple's piece sold for $69 million and added more information to the climate change section.

Update March 15th, 1:30PM ET: Added a link to our piece on the environmental impact of NFTs and updated some of the language to reflect some recent research. Also added a poem.

Beeple sold an NFT for $69 million

Until October, the most Mike Winkelmann — the digital artist known as Beeple — had ever sold a print for was $100.

Today, an NFT of his work sold for $69 million at Christie's. The sale positions him "among the top three most valuable living artists," according to the auction house.

The record-smashing NFT sale comes after months of increasingly valuable auctions. In October, Winkelmann sold his first series of NFTs, with a pair going for $66,666.66 each. In December, he sold a series of works for $3.5 million total. And last month, one of the NFTs that originally sold for $66,666.66 was resold for $6.6 million.

"I DO VIEW THIS AS THE NEXT CHAPTER OF ART HISTORY."

NFTs, or non-fungible tokens, are unique files that live on a blockchain and are able to verify ownership of a work of digital art. Buyers typically get limited rights to display the digital artwork they represent, but in many ways, they're just buying bragging rights and an asset they may be able to resell later. The technology has absolutely exploded over the past few weeks — and Winkelmann, more than anyone else, has been at the forefront of its rapid rise.

"He showed us this collage, and that was my eureka moment when I knew this was going to be extremely important," Noah Davis, a specialist in post-war and contemporary art at Christie's, told *The Verge*. "It was just so monumental and so indicative of what NFTs can do."

A few factors explain why Beeple's work has become so valuable. For one, he's developed a large fan base, with around 2.5 million followers across social channels. And he's famously prolific: as part of a project called "Everydays," Winkelmann creates and publishes a new digital artwork *every day*. The project is now in its 14th year.

At the same time, NFTs have blown up over the past month and — for the moment, at least — are being seen by many as *the way* digital art will be acquired and traded going forward. For collectors who believe that's true, the escalating prices are nothing compared to what NFTs will be worth down the road, when the rest of the world has caught onto their value.

Christie's is also a legitimizing force for both Winkelmann's art and NFTs as a technology. The 255-year-old auction house has sold some of the most famous paintings in history, from the only known portrait of Shakespeare created during his lifetime to the last-discovered painting by Leonardo da Vinci.

NFTs Are Booming, But They're Nothing New in the Art Market

Four months after Pablo Rodriguez-Fraile spent nearly $67,000 on a digital artwork of Joe Biden and Donald Trump in the nude, the piece had transformed. Designed to respond to election results, it had morphed into a naked, graffiti-covered Donald Trump lying on a trash-strewn lawn. The price changed, too: Rodriguez-

Fraile sold it for $6.6 million. "Obviously, I thought it would take a bit longer" to appreciate in value, says the 32-year-old with an MBA from Columbia, who describes himself as a digital asset investor. "Having said that, funnily enough, I actually think it was a fantastic deal for the buyer."

The work in question is a short video created by Mike Winkelmann, an artist who goes by Beeple. But what Rodriguez-Fraile sold was not an everyday video file. The art is attached to something called a nonfungible token, or NFT. Like the cryptocurrency Bitcoin, NFTs run on blockchain technology. Unlike Bitcoins, each NFT can be a unique digital property—one NFT can represent ownership of a specific work of art. It can also be designed to suit a creator's needs: NFTs connected to Beeple's artworks, for instance, give him a 10% royalty every time his art changes hands. Far more important, Beeple's NFTs have his signature and proof of sale built into their code. There's no way to fake or forge or replicate one of his artworks, at least as long as the NFT is considered integral to the work.

NFTs' ability to confer uniqueness has led to a boom in digital art's collectibility. Before, anyone could replicate an image an infinite number of times, making it impossible to create the perception of scarcity or value. There was no way, in other words, to build a market. NFTs offered a solution. There could be infinite JPEG files of an artwork, but only one "real" image specified by the NFT. Or six. Or 100. Whatever edition size the artwork's creator specified was what it would be. With an almost literal flip of the switch, a market was born.

relates to NFTs Are Booming, But They're Nothing New in the Art Market

Infected Culture, digital art by Beeple.

There is a tendency to compare the boom in NFTs with the rally in GameStop shares, another recent, jaw-dropping value creation story that also seemed, to outsiders at least, to have come from nowhere. It's a particularly seductive narrative because the same people—young, tech-savvy men—appear to be behind both phenomena. But there's a big difference. Critics of GameStop buyers say the stocks became detached from the company's fundamentals: A stock price is supposed to reflect things like profit, earnings, and assets.

This is not how the art market works, and it's not how it has ever worked. Paintings aren't valued based on the price of the paint used on the canvas, and Jeff Koons's Rabbit sculpture didn't sell for $91 million at Christie's because of the amount of steel used to make it. (The sculpture is 41 inches high.) Art prices might rise and fall, but not because of fundamentals; instead, consensus alone confers value.

A good example—and a precedent for NFTs—is the development of the photography market. Like digital art, a photograph can be reproduced over and over and over from its original negative. Yet despite that reproducibility, not all prints are priced accordingly. "The market has always had ways in which to maintain value," says Geoffrey Batchen, a professor of art history at the University of Oxford who recently published the book Negative/ Positive: A History of Photography.

Consider, Batchen suggests, Ansel Adams's 1941 photograph Moonrise, Hernandez, New Mexico. "He made at least 1,300 and possibly more prints from that negative," Batchen says. "But if you look at auction catalogs, they will carefully parse which were the 'better' ones: which were printed by Adams alone, which were signed by Adams, which were made for portfolios."

relates to NFTs Are Booming, But They're Nothing New in the Art Market

Beeple's digital art kit with physical coin included.

To be clear, the image is the same, though Adams kept adjusting prints' contrast and size. But it's Adams's signature or other minor distinctions that delineate a $50,000 print from one that's worth $650,000. "There is no logic to it other than the need to maintain capital," Batchen says. "It's entirely a market conception imposed on this object."

While this distinction might be lost on outsiders, many NFT collectors are willing to spend huge sums, at least in part, to impose and normalize a similar market framework for digital art. Before NFTs, "digital artists haven't really gotten what they deserve," says Tim Kang, a 27-year-old who says he's spent about $1 million on almost 200 digital artworks. "It's just one of the most artistic mediums, and [digital artists] do work for others, and they don't get any recognition for it, hardly."

Kang was dragged into the spotlight in January, when he spent a then-record $777,777 (and 77¢) on a collection of artworks by Beeple. "It was hard for me to process at the time" why he'd made such a big purchase, he says. Only later did he realize, he says, that "I wanted to ensure that this is valid, that this is the future. I was taking a stand for our future of creative liberation."

A finance-minded skeptic might say the NFTs' success is a product of the cryptocurrency boom, meaning there are lots of people sitting on fortunes in digital tokens looking for something to buy. But that's hardly different from the way a bull market in stocks can push up the auction price of a Picasso.

Batchen says the emergence of NFTs represents both the future and the past of the art market. "There's a continuity here, across the history of art," he says. "Especially when you come to media that are capable of multiple reproductions like prints and photographs and digital images." The real issue, he says, "is not the artificialness or otherwise of the value of digital objects. It's can they survive the obsolescence of the medium that conveys them?" In other words, are hard drives and blockchain technology as durable as well-preserved canvas and oil paint?

Rodriguez-Fraile, who says he's spent seven figures on digital art, isn't worried. "Are these going to be here in 500 years? That's a potential concern," he says. "I'm sure that something will happen along the way and some [digital art] will get lost. But it will certainly be a lower percentage than the physical art that's created in the world."

Standards For Nfts

Before we delve into the history of nun-fungible tokens and how they came into being, it is imperative to know and understand the 'standards' that these NFTs have. Standards play a monumental role when it comes to making non-fungible tokens powerful. In the case of NFTs, standards give developers a certain level of guarantee or assurance that the assets involved will behave in a specific way. These standards also describe how interactions will work when they try to interact with the assets' basic functionality.

ERC721

This is the most popular standard when it comes to non-fungible tokens and was pioneered by none other than Cryptokitties. It is a blockchain game developed on Ethereum. This unique game allows the players to purchase, collect, breed, and sell virtual cats. Cryptokitties is an important landmark in the history of NFTs because they portray one of the earliest attempts made to employ blockchain for leisure activities. This is how ERC721 became the first standard ever that represented non-fungible digital assets. It is an inheritable Solidarity smart contract, which implies that interested and involved developers can create fresh and new ERC721-compliant contracts with ease by simply importing them from the OpenZepplin library.

ERC721 involves two relatively simple methods that also reflect the essence of an NFT. The first is that it provides a mapping of unique identifiers to addresses. These represent the owner of the aforementioned identifier. Secondly, it also provides an authorized and permissioned way to transfer these assets. This is also known as the 'transferFrom' method. This is the core of the ERC721 standard for non-fungible tokens.

ERC1155

The Enjin team developed this non-fungible token standard. What's unique about this Ethereum standard is that it brings the idea of semi-fungibility into the NFT world. With this standard, IDs represent a class of assets instead of individual assets. A major advantage of this system is that it brings efficiency and reduces the efforts to modify smart contracts for a large number of items. This makes development work significantly easier. Developers can carry out large modifications in the smart contracts with simple changes. However, this does not come without the loss of information as the history and information of individual assets cannot be traced.

Non-Ethereum Standards

Non-Ethereum standards are pioneered by chains other than Ethereum, with one of the most prominent examples being DGoods. This standard is pioneered by the Mythical Games team starting with EOS and focuses on providing a feature-rich and heavy cross-chain standard. Another notable development is the emergence of the Cosmos project, which is developing an NFT module that can be leveraged as a part of the Cosmos SDK.

Non-fungible tokens: a brief history

Now that we have a basic idea about how non-fungible tokens work and the standards involved, we can delve into how they came into being. Before Cryprokitties, a period that is unironically known as '0 BC', some experiments began with the emergence of colored coins in the Bitcoin network. Illustrations known as 'Rare Pepe' that was built on the Bitcoin counterparty system were one of the first few, and some of these illustrations were sold on eBay. Later, a rare set of Rare Pepe was even sold in an auction in New York.

CryptoPunks became the first Ethereum-based non-fungible token experiment, and it consisted of 10,000 unique punk collectibles, with each of them having individual and unique characteristics and features. This was built by Larva Labs and was featured as an on-chain marketplace that could be accessed and used by crypto wallets such as MetaMask. This further lowered the barrier to entry to interact with non-fungible tokens for crypto users. Today, CyberPunks are, in essence, true digital antiques, and since they live on Ethereum, it makes them interoperable with wallets and marketplaces.

Cryptokitties mark the beginning of an era which pushed NFTs into the mainstream and were launched in late 2017. Cryptokitties debuted at the ETH Waterloo hackathon with a primitive on-chain game. Many in the gaming community labeled them as 'not a real game', but the team found their way around the blockchain's design constraints considerably well.

This project was covered by all major platforms, from CNN to CoindDesk, due to two main reasons: the game was slowing down the Ethereum network, and people were making insane profits while trading them. Some virtual cats even sold for over $100,000! This rise of NFTs, thanks to CryptoKitties, coincided with the 2017 crypto bull market, which encouraged people to participate extensively. It was one reason why people opened up to the idea of non-fungible tokens and looked into their incredible potential. Dapper Labs, a company created by Axiom Zen, the genius behind CryptoKitties, successfully received a whopping $15 million funding from top investors such as Google Ventures.

The period between 2018 and 2019 is known for the NFT Cambrian Explosion, which resulted in both these years witnessing a massive and exponential growth of non-fungible tokens. Although smaller in volume compared to other crypto markets, the trade volumes are growing at a brisk rate and have a long way to go. With the emergence of websites such as nonfungible.com and nftcryptonews.com, which provide ample generic information about the space while also delving into the specifics about the NFT market metrics and gameplay guides, NFTs are now more accessible and easy to learn about than ever before.

Salient features of blockchain-based NFTs

When non-fungible tokens and blockchain technology come together, they make something powerful, unique, and interesting for users and developers that utilize them. While we have already discussed that non-fungible assets are all around us, the real problem is the part where ownership comes up. This is where Blockchain saves the day- it provides a coordination layer for digital assets. In layman's terms, it gives users all permissions regarding ownership and management of these digital assets. Here are some salient features of blockchain-based non-fungible tokens:

Standardization

Standardization is a revolutionary feature for NFTs because the emergence of digital assets, from domain names to airplane tickets, has no unified representation in the digital world. However, when NFTs are represented on public blockchains, they allow developers to build common, inheritable, and reusable standards relevant to all NFTs. This standardization serves as building blocks for digital assets from basic ownership, transfer, and control to advanced features such as additional standards for displaying the NFTs.

Traceability

The interoperability of NFTs, which we will discuss in the next section, paves the way for one of the most compelling features of NFTs, known as the traceability that enables free trade in open markets. This means that users can trade items outside of their original environments and transfer them to a place where they can leverage sophisticated trading systems and technologies. These include bidding, bundling, eBay-style auctions, the feature to trade in any currency, and many more. This traceability represents a shift from a closed economy to an open and free-market economy, specifically for game developers.

Interoperability

The NFT standards allow the easy and free movement of NFTs across various ecosystems and make them accessible inside several wallet providers if a new NFT project is launched. By making them displayable inside of virtual worlds, they become tradeable on a plethora of marketplaces. This interoperability is widely credited to open standards, which enable and provide consistent, clear, and reliable API that is authorized and permissioned for writing and reading data.

Liquidity

When NFTs are instantly tradeable, it paves the way for higher liquidity. This implies that the non-fungible token marketplaces will be able to cater to a wide variety of audiences, which will allow better and far greater exposure of these assets for a larger pool of buyers. These can include experienced and hardcore traders and even novice players who have just ventured into this arena. Hence, in a way, NFTs are expanding the market and demand for unique digital assets worldwide.

Immutability and provable scarcity

Non-fungible tokens use smart contracts that also allow developers to place hard caps on their supply. Additionally, it empowers developers to enforce stringent and persistent properties that cannot be changed or modified after issuing these non-fungible tokens. Moreover, the developers can also specify which properties cannot be modified over time by encoding them on-chain. Hence, this is crucial and beneficial for several digital assets, including art, which relies heavily on individual pieces' provable scarcity.

Programmability

Finally, another interesting characteristic of blockchain-based non-fungible tokens is the fact that they are highly programmable. A prominent example is that of CyptoKitties, who baked in a breeding mechanic into the actual contract directly, which represented digital cats. Moreover, several non-fungible tokens today have more intricate and complicated mechanics that include redeeming, random generation, crafting, forging, and much more, proving that this space is full of infinite potential and great possibilities.

Where can NFTs be used?

NFTs have a wide range of applications since they exist and trade on the blockchain network. Here are a few ways through which you can use NFTs!

Construct and curate collections

Showcase your public non-fungible token inventory through various means such as social media or decentralized applications

Use non-fungible tokens in games and other decentralized applications

Gift and/or trade NFTs with other people

Purchase NFTs in a marketplace

Buy NFTs in a marketplace

The future of Non-fungible tokens

Non-fungible tokens are extremely new, and the technology behind them is still undergoing significant changes and improvements through tireless innovations. They come with their own sets of challenges and limitations that need to be tackled for smoother incorporation and usage. The first obstacle is that they are very inaccessible to mainstream users, in the sense that currently, only early tech adopters and spectators are using blockchain platforms.

The second obstacle boils down to purchasing and selling non-fungible tokens and building efficient applications that can support larger transactions. However, the future looks promising for NFTs as the total market for them crossed a whopping $100 million by the end of July 2020. Experts in the crypto industry even speculate that 40% of new crypto users will use NFTs as an entry point. With the decentralized finance industry surpassing $4 billion in value, it is evident that the NFT space is set to grow exponentially in the days to come.

How to Create, Buy and Sell NFTs

NFTs have become one of the hottest crypto trends of 2021, with overall sales up 55% already since 2020, from **$250 million to $389 million.** Here's how you can create, purchase and sell these popular digitals assets.

Non-fungible tokens (NFTs), which are unique collectible crypto assets, have been around as early as 2012 when the concept of Bitcoin Colored Coins first emerged. These coins were simply satoshis – small fractions of a bitcoin – marked, or "colored in" with distinct information that could link the coins to real-world assets, such as "this satoshi represents $500 of John Doe's New York office building." For the most part, however, Colored Coins were used to create and trade artwork like "Rare Pepe" digital cards on Counterparty, a peer-to-peer trading platform built on top of Bitcoin's blockchain.

These cartoon frog images adapted from a viral internet meme were some of the earliest examples of unique digital artwork tied to crypto tokens. This paved the way for the ideation and creation of new non-fungible token standards – a set of blockchain building blocks that allow developers to create their own NFTs.

NFTs can be used to represent virtually any type of real or intangible item, including:

Artwork

Virtual items within video games such as skins, virtual currency, weapons and avatars

Music

Collectibles (e.g. digital trading cards)

Tokenized real-world assets, from real estate and cars to racehorses and designer sneakers

Virtual land

Video footage of iconic sporting moments

How to create NFTs

Creating your own NFT artwork, whether it be a GIF or an image, is a relatively straightforward process and doesn't require extensive knowledge of the crypto industry. NFT artwork can also be used to create collectibles like sets of digital cards.

Before you start, you will need to decide on which blockchain you want to issue your NFTs. Ethereum is currently the leading blockchain service for NFT issuance. However, there is a range of other blockchains that are becoming increasingly popular, including:

- Binance Smart Chain
- Flow by Dapper Labs
- Tron
- EOS
- Polkadot
- Tezos
- Cosmos

- WAX

Each blockchain has its own separate NFT token standard, compatible wallet services and marketplaces. For instance, if you create NFTs on top of the Binance Smart Chain, you will only be able to sell them on platforms that support Binance Smart Chain assets. This means you wouldn't be able to sell them on something like VIV3 – a Flow blockchain-based marketplace – or OpenSea which is an Ethereum-based NFT marketplace.

Since Ethereum has the largest NFT ecosystem, here's what you'll need to mint your own NFT artwork, music or video on the Ethereum blockchain:

An Ethereum wallet that supports ERC-721 (the Ethereum-based NFT token standard), such as MetaMask, Trust Wallet or Coinbase Wallet.

Around $50-$100 in ether (ETH). If you are using Coinbase's wallet you can buy ether from the platform with U.S. dollars, British pound sterling and other fiat currencies. Otherwise, you will need to purchase ether from a cryptocurrency exchange.

Once you have these, there are a number of NFT-centric platforms that allow you to connect your wallet and upload your chosen image or file that you want to turn into an NFT.

The main Ethereum NFT marketplaces include:

- OpenSea
- Rarible
- Mintable

Makersplace also allows you to create your own NFTs but you have to register to become a listed artist on the platform beforehand.

OpenSea, Rarible and Mintable all have a "create" button in the top right corner.

Here's how the process works on OpenSea, currently the largest Ethereum-based NFT marketplace.

OpenSea NFT marketplace built on Ethereum

Clicking the "create" button will take you to a screen that asks you to connect your Ethereum-based wallet. Once you've entered your wallet password when requested it will automatically connect your wallet with the marketplace. You may have to digitally sign a message in your Ethereum wallet to prove you own the wallet address, but it's just a case of clicking through to proceed.

Digitally signing a message does not incur a fee, it's just to show that you have ownership over the wallet.

The next step on OpenSea is to hover over "create" in the top right corner and select "my collections." From there, click the blue "create" button as shown below.

Creating an NFT collection on OpenSea

A window will appear that allows you to upload your artwork, add a name and include a description.

This part is essentially just you creating a folder for your newly created NFTs to go in.

OpenSea NFT collection creation window

Once you've assigned an image for your collection, it will appear as shown below (blue). You'll then need to add a banner image to the page by clicking on the pencil icon in the top right corner (red).

Your page should end up looking something like the image below.

Now, you're ready to create your first NFT. Click on the "Add New Item" button (blue) and sign another message using your wallet.

Creating NFT collection on OpenSea(

You'll arrive at a new window where you can upload your NFT image, audio, GIF or 3D model.

On OpenSea and many other marketplaces, you also have the option to include special traits and attributes to increase the scarcity and uniqueness of your NFT. Creators even have the opportunity to include unlockable content that can only be viewed by the purchaser. This can be anything from passwords to access certain services to discount codes and contact information.

Once you're finished, click "create" at the bottom and sign another message in your wallet to confirm the creation of the NFT. The artwork should then appear in your collection.

How much does it cost to make NFTs?

While it costs nothing to make NFTs on OpenSea, some platforms charge a fee. With Ethereum-based platforms, this fee is known as "gas." Ethereum gas is simply an amount of ether required to perform a certain function on the blockchain – in this instance, it would be adding a new NFT to the marketplace. The cost of gas varies depending on network congestion. The higher the number of people transacting value over the network at a given time, the higher the price of gas fees and vice versa.

Top tip: Ethereum gas fees are significantly cheaper on average during the weekend when fewer people are transacting value over the network. This can help keep costs down if you're listing multiple NFTs for sale.

How to sell NFTs

To sell your NFTs on a marketplace, you'll need to locate them in your collection, click on them and find the "sell" button. Clicking this will take you to a pricing page where you can define the conditions of the sale including whether to run an auction or sell at a fixed price.

Ether and other ERC-20 tokens are the most common cryptocurrencies you can sell your NFTs for, however, some platforms only support the native token of the blockchain they were built upon. VIV3, for example, is a Flow blockchain marketplace and only accepts FLOW tokens.

By clicking on the "edit" button next to the collection image on OpenSea, signing the message using your wallet and scrolling down, you have the option to program in royalties and select which ERC-20 token you'd like to receive for selling the NFT. Royalties allow NFT creators to earn a commission every time the asset is sold to a new person. This has the potential to create lifelong passive income streams for artists and other content creators automatically thanks to smart contracts.

Selling NFTs on OpenSea

Listing NFTs on a marketplace sometimes requires a fee in order to complete the process. While it's not the case with every platform, it's something to be mindful of when creating NFTs.

How to buy NFTs

Before you rush to buy NFTs, there are four things you need to consider first:

What marketplace do you intend to buy the NFTs from?

What wallet do you need to download in order to connect with the platform and purchase NFTs?

Which cryptocurrency do you need to fund the wallet with in order to complete the sale?

Are the NFTs you want to buy being sold at a specific time, i.e. via a pack or art drop?

As you can probably guess by now, certain NFTs are only available on specific platforms. For example, if you want to purchase <u>NBA Top Shot</u> packs you will need to open an account with NBA Top Shot, create a Dapper wallet and fund it with either the <u>USDC stablecoin</u> or supported fiat currency options. You will also have to wait for one of the card pack drops to be announced and try your luck in trying to buy them before they sell out.

Pack and art drops are becoming increasingly common as a method for selling scarce NFTs to an audience of hungry buyers. These drops normally require users to sign up and fund their accounts beforehand so that they don't miss out on the opportunity to purchase NFTs when they drop. Pack and art drops can be over in seconds, so you need to have everything ready ahead of time.

Where to buy NFTs

For crypto traders who are primarily interested in buying NFTs, here is a list of the most popular NFT marketplaces in 2021:

- OpenSea
- Rarible
- SuperRare
- Nifty Gateway
- Foundation
- Axie Marketplace
- BakerySwap
- NFT ShowRoom
- VIV3

Is now a good time to get into non-fungible tokens?

The NFT craze is far from being over. Major brands and celebrities such as the UFC and Shawn Mendez have signed deals to release their own non-fungible assets soon, and even Elon Musk's girlfriend Grimes has jumped on the bandwagon selling almost $6 million worth of digital artwork in minutes.

Messari analyst Mason Nystrom anticipates the NFT market will exceed $1.3 billion by the end of 2021 as more artists, brands and icons flock to the space to create their own distinctive tokens. With more blockchains competing to produce better NFT services too and a growing range of platforms to choose from, now is a great time to take part in the space.

Lightning Source UK Ltd.
Milton Keynes UK
UKHW020640010421
381372UK00011B/884